Blue Moon Valley is a small village. Li Sun lives there
with her grandmother. She is very happy in Blue Moon
Valley. But there is a problem. Li Sun's grandmother is
very old and very ill. She cannot work any more and
has no money. One bright April morning she says to Li
Sun, "Sit down, granddaughter. I have something to
tell you."

Barcode at back →

"What is it, grandmother?" asks Li Sun. The old woman's eyes are sad and tired. "Read this letter," she says. "It's for your uncle in the big city. I want you to go and talk to him." Li Sun reads the letter. "But ... " she says and looks at her grandmother. "You're asking him to give me a job ... in his circus!"

"Yes," the old woman answers.

Li Sun and her grandmother talk for a long time. Li
Sun does not want to leave Blue Moon Valley. "It's my
home!" she says. "But every child leaves home one
day," the old woman answers. "And you're not a child
now – you're a young woman. I want you to be free."
In the end, Li Sun looks at the floor and says, "Yes,
grandmother." Two days later she leaves the village.

In the next week Li Sun walks a long way. She sees
mountains, fields, trees and farms. Every morning she
drinks from cold rivers. Every night she sleeps under
thousands of bright stars. Then after eight days, she
comes to the big city. It has high walls with stone lions
on top of them. Hundreds of people are running left
and right in front of her.

"Excuse me," she says to an old man. "Do you know this address?" She shows him her grandmother's letter.

"You want the circus," he says. "That's easy. Go down this street and turn left at the end."

Ten minutes later Li Sun is at the circus.

Her uncle is very happy to see her. "Yes – of *course* you can have a job," he says. "Come with me."

Behind the circus there are some big cages. "Here
we are," says Li Sun's uncle. "You can help to wash the
animals." He smiles. "And you can help to give them
their food, too. Do you understand?"

Li Sun looks at all the animals. There are monkeys,
tigers, elephants, horses and lions. Then she looks at
her uncle again. "Y-yes, Uncle," she says.

Li Sun works very hard for three months. Every week she writes to her grandmother. In her letters she says, "I'm very happy." But she is not. She tells her only friend, Choo Choo the panda, "I want to go home." Then one day her uncle says, "The Emperor is coming here tomorrow. I want all the animals to be very, *very* clean. All right?" "Of course," says Li Sun.

The next morning Li Sun is giving the tigers their food.
Suddenly she hears her uncle say, "You've got another
job?" She opens the long, red curtains. Her uncle is
talking to Yu Mei. She works with Wu Chi, the
horseman. "Yes," says Yu Mei. "And I'm leaving today.
Goodbye." After she leaves, Li Sun's uncle looks at Wu
Chi. "*Now* what can we do?" he asks.

A moment later he sees Li Sun. "Of course!" he says. "Li
Sun. *She* can help you this evening." "What?!" Wu Chi
laughs. "But she can't learn Yu Mei's job in one day."
"Do you have another answer?" asks Li Sun's uncle. Wu
Chi says nothing.

In ten minutes, Li Sun is wearing Yu Mei's circus
clothes.

That evening the Emperor arrives at seven o'clock. He
is wearing beautiful gold clothes. He sits down and
watches the circus. Then at the end he talks to Li Sun's
uncle. "Who is that new girl with your horseman?" he
asks. "Her name is Li Sun," comes the answer. The
Emperor smiles. "She is young, but very good." "Oh,
thank you, Emperor," says Li Sun's uncle.

After that evening, Li Sun does not clean the animals'
cages any more. She works with Wu Chi every day. But
that is not all. She starts to love the horseman, too.
They often walk in a beautiful park next to the
Emperor's palace. There, one day in October, Wu Chi
puts a hand on Li Sun's arm. "You make me very
happy," he says. "I want you to be my wife."

Li Sun does not know what to say. She wants to be Wu
Chi's wife, but . . . not here in the big city. She wants to
live with him at home in Blue Moon Valley. She tells
him this and looks into his eyes. "Can you understand?"
she asks. Wu Chi looks down. "I don't know," he
answers. "*My* home is here in the city. Let me think
about it. We can talk again tomorrow."

It is a very long night for Li Sun. She cannot sleep. She
goes to see her old friend, Choo Choo. "Oh – what's he
going to say tomorrow?" she asks the panda. "Am I
doing the right thing? I love him, but I *can't* live in the
city. I don't like it. My home's back in Blue Moon
Valley." Choo Choo looks at Li Sun. His eyes are big,
brown and sad.

Early next morning, Wu Chi finds Li Sun in the
panda's cage. "Come with me," he says.
They go to see Li Sun's uncle. Wu Chi has something
to tell him. "Li Sun's going to be my wife," he says,
"but that's not all. We're leaving the circus. I'm going
to be a farmer in Blue Moon Valley."
"Oh, Wu Chi!" says Li Sun. She is very, very happy.

One week later Li Sun and Wu Chi leave the city.
Everyone comes to say goodbye. Then, at the last
minute, four men arrive. They are carrying a big box.
"What's this?" asks Li Sun. "It's something from all of
us," says her uncle. "Please open it." Li Sun opens the
box. "*Choo Choo*!" she says. "Oh uncle, thank you.
Thank you!"

Questions

1 Why does Li Sun leave Blue Moon Valley? (*page 3*)

2 How many days does it take her to get to the big city? (*page 4*)

3 Which animals sit on top of the city walls? (*page 4*)

4 What is Li Sun's first job at her uncle's circus? (*page 6*)

5 Why does Yu Mei suddenly leave? (*page 8*)

6 What time does the Emperor arrive? (*page 10*)

7 Where do Li Sun and Wu Chi often walk? (*page 11*)

8 What is Wu Chi going to do in Blue Moon Valley? (*page 14*)

9 What does Li Sun's uncle give her? (*page 15*)

Puzzle

How many English words can you make from the letters in BLUE MOON VALLEY? Here are four to help you start:

ball/many/love/meal

Ideas

1 Paint a poster. Call it *An Evening at the Circus.* Put in Li Sun, Wu Chi, Li Sun's uncle, the Emperor, Choo Choo, and lots of animals. Include the names of all the animals and people in your poster.

2 Write a letter from Li Sun or Wu Chi to Li Sun's uncle. It is one year after the end of the story. What is happening in Blue Moon Valley?

KA 0277940 4